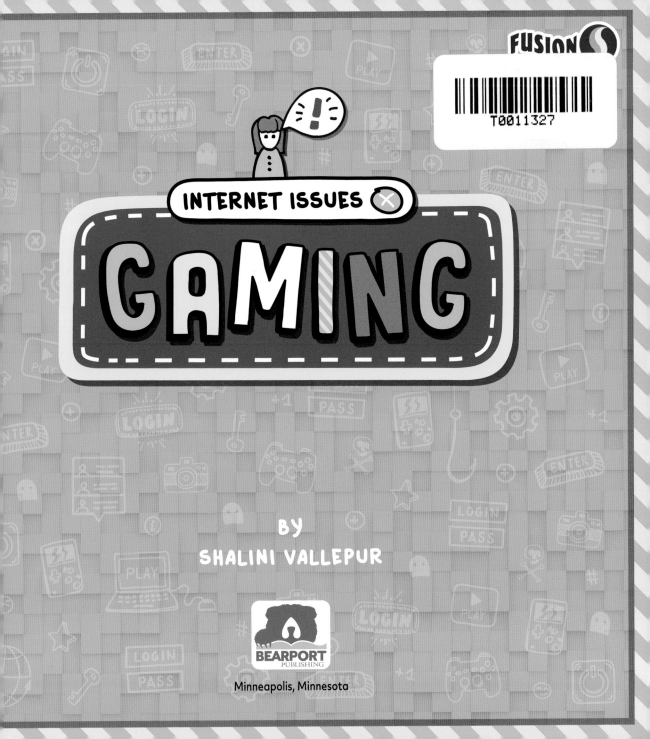

FUSION

T0011327

INTERNET ISSUES

GAMING

BY
SHALINI VALLEPUR

BEARPORT
PUBLISHING

Minneapolis, Minnesota

Credits
All images are courtesy of Shutterstock.com, unless otherwise specified. With thanks to Getty Images, Thinkstock Photo, and iStockphoto. Front Cover – Anton27, BlurryMe, Monkey Busines. Images used on every page – Bloomicon, Alex Maen CG. 2 – BlurryMe. 4–5 – adriaticfoto, giuseppelombardo. 6–7 – Creativa Images, fizkes. 8–9 – 4 PM production, Aayan Arts, emodpk, BlurryMe.10–11 – AnnGaysorn, ESB Professional, Kekyalyaynen, sakkmesterke, Siam Stock. 12–13 – fizkes, Kiselev Andrey Valerevich, Kleber Cordeiro, TheVisualsYouNeed. 14–15 – mama_mia, Tero Vesalainen. 16–17 – Alex Tihonovs, Prostock-studio, Sergey Maksienko. 18–19 – asiandeligh, junpinzon, Syda Productions. 20–21 – bbernard, namtipStudio, Prostock-studio, Rawpixel.com. 22–23 – jamesteohart, Syda Productions.

Bearport Publishing Company Product Development Team
President: Jen Jenson; Director of Product Development: Spencer Brinker; Managing Editor: Allison Juda; Associate Editor: Naomi Reich; Associate Editor: Tiana Tran; Senior Designer: Colin O'Dea; Associate Designer: Elena Klinkner; Associate Designer: Kayla Eggert; Product Development Specialist: Anita Stasson

Library of Congress Cataloging-in-Publication Data is available at www.loc.gov or upon request from the publisher.

ISBN: 979-8-88509-962-2 (hardcover)
ISBN: 979-8-88822-138-9 (paperback)
ISBN: 979-8-88822-282-9 (ebook)

For more information, write to Bearport Publishing, 5357 Penn Avenue South, Minneapolis, MN 55419.

CONTENTS

THE INTERNET

Have you ever been on the internet? It connects the world's computers, smartphones, and gaming **consoles**.

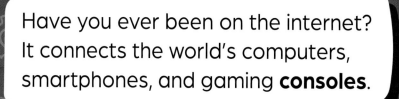

People all over the world use the internet every day. They use it to work, to learn, to play, and even to talk with other people.

ONLINE

Many video games can be played over the internet. This is called online gaming. Often, these games are played with others.

ALWAYS ASK A GROWN-UP BEFORE YOU PLAY ONLINE.

Online gaming can be a lot of fun. But there are things to think about before playing online.

DIFFERENT ✕ DEVICES

There are many different types of online games. They can be played on different **devices** and game consoles.

A GAME CONTROLLER AND CONSOLE

A HANDHELD GAME CONSOLE

CONSOLES CAN BE CONNECTED
TO TELEVISIONS TO PLAY
GAMES ON BIG SCREENS.

HANDHELD GAME CONSOLES
HAVE THEIR OWN SCREENS.

COMPUTER GAMES ARE PLAYED ON COMPUTERS AND LAPTOPS.

A LAPTOP

A COMPUTER

!?!

A SMARTPHONE

10

A TABLET

GAMING **APPS** CAN BE PLAYED ON SMARTPHONES AND TABLETS.

HAVE YOU PLAYED GAMES ON ANY OF THESE DEVICES?

HOW OLD ⊗ ARE YOU?

Games usually have an age rating. It tells how old a player should be to play.

A 3+ AGE RATING MEANS ANYONE WHO IS THREE OR OLDER CAN PLAY.

3+

IT IS IMPORTANT TO PLAY GAMES ONLY IF THEY ARE MADE FOR YOUR AGE.

ALWAYS CHECK WITH A GROWN-UP IF YOU ARE UNSURE ABOUT A GAME'S RATING.

There are lots of reasons a game is given an older age rating. Some games may show things that can make us feel unsafe or upset.

PERSONAL ⊗ INFORMATION

To play online games, you usually need to make an **account**. The game may want you to set up a username and password. It might also ask for your personal information.

USERNAME

BIRTHDAY

NEVER SHARE PERSONAL INFORMATION OR YOUR REAL NAME WITH OTHER GAMERS.

ADDRESS

REAL NAME

EMAIL ADDRESS

A USERNAME IS A MADE-UP NAME OTHER PLAYERS CAN SEE.

BEING SMART WHILE PICKING YOUR USERNAME AND PASSWORD CAN KEEP YOU SAFE ONLINE.

USERNAME: RODBARKMAN

PASSWORD: TOPDOG4EVA

Login

A PASSWORD SHOULD BE HARD FOR OTHER PEOPLE TO GUESS.

A username should be fun! But it should not include any personal information. Don't use your real name or where you live.

GAMES

Online games are often multiplayer games. This means you may be able to talk to other players with a **microphone** or type messages to them in a chat box.

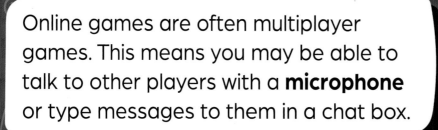

RODBARKMAN:
ARE YOU PLAYING THE NEXT GAME?

2FAST2SONIC:
YES!

RODBARKMAN:
GREAT! WE MAKE A GOOD TEAM.

2FAST2SONIC:
LET'S WIN THIS GAME!

It can be hard to know who you are playing with online. When possible, stick to playing with people you know in real life.

ALWAYS TELL A GROWN-UP WHEN YOU ARE PLAYING ONLINE GAMES WITH OTHER PEOPLE.

CYBERBULLYING

Cyberbullying can happen over the internet. People might say mean things they would not say in person.

Always be kind to people on the internet. If you see cyberbullying, tell a grown-up.

APPS

With gaming apps, you can play games almost anywhere. However, sometimes you can **accidentally** spend money.

CLICK HERE TO PAY!

BE CAREFUL ON GAMING APPS, AND TELL A GROWN-UP IF YOU BUY SOMETHING BY MISTAKE.

Some gaming apps try to trick players into spending money. Make sure you keep an eye out. If you're getting extra stuff in a game, it could come with a fee.

SAFE GAMING

Now you know all about online gaming! Let's review how to stay safe when you play games online.

KNOW HOW TO BLOCK OTHER PLAYERS.

NEVER SHARE YOUR PERSONAL INFORMATION WITH OTHER GAMERS.

ALWAYS BE KIND TO OTHER PLAYERS.

WATCH OUT FOR IN-GAME CHARGES.

MAKE SURE A GROWN-UP KNOWS WHEN YOU ARE PLAYING ONLINE GAMES.

MAKE YOUR USERNAME DIFFERENT FROM YOUR REAL NAME.

PLAY GAMES THAT ARE THE RIGHT AGE FOR YOU.

GLOSSARY

accidentally happening by mistake

account a login for a website or game that connects with information about you

apps things on phones or tablets that do different tasks

block to stop messages or contact from another person

consoles devices that are used to play video games

cyberbullying posting mean messages about a person online

devices machines such as tablets, smartphones, and computers

microphone a thing that is spoken into so that others far away can hear

INDEX